BRIAN RIDER

BIRD'S EYE
PERSPECTIVE
DRAWING
MINI GUIDES 2016

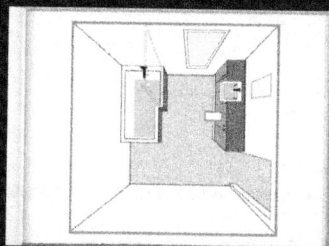

01

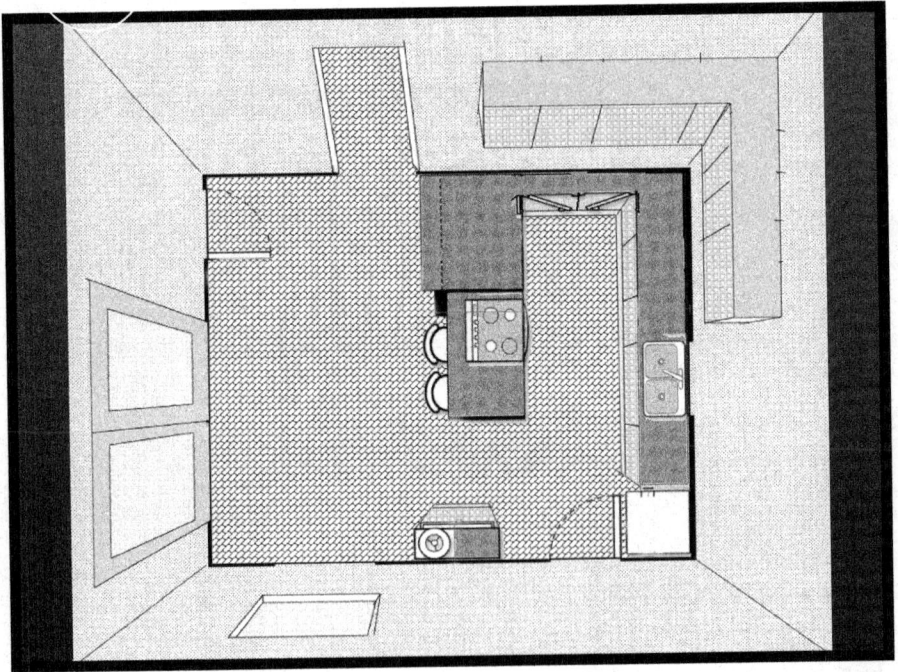

BIRD'S EYE PERSPECTIVE

THE VANISHING POINT

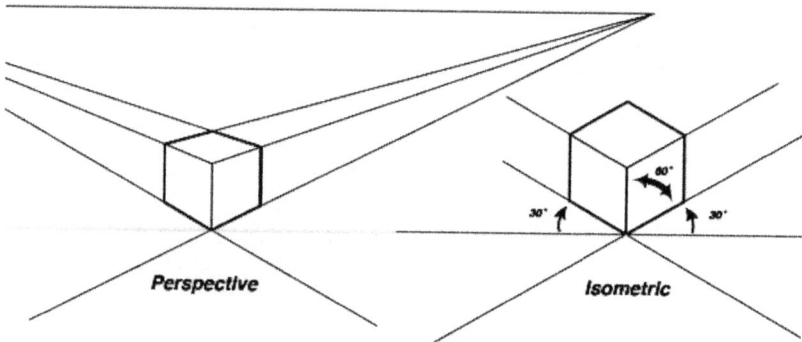

Perspective   Isometric

"

THE WHOLE SECRET OF PERSPECTIVE DRAWING WAS THE DISCOVERY OF THE VANISHING POINT. BEFORE THAT ARTISTS WERE NOT ABLE TO ILLUSTRATE DISTANCE

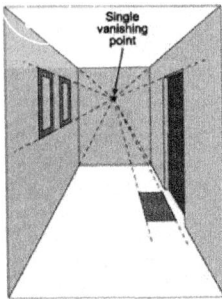

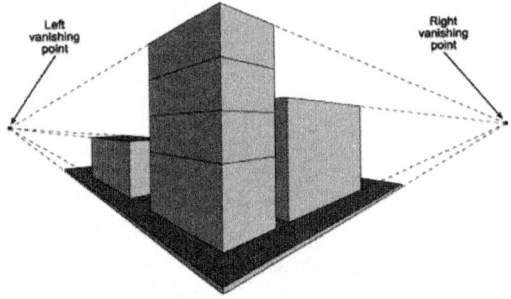

Single vanishing point

Left vanishing point

Right vanishing point

VANISHING POINT

Just a point to remember - the 2 point perspective on the right hand shows the corner edge of a building or box. In the case of interior design you will be looking at the back corner of the room - therefore the lines will be drawn from the vanishing point to the opposite wall. The vanishing point in bird's eye perspective is like drawing one seen directly from above turning the drawing on it's back.

VANISHING POINT IN BIRD'S EYE

BIRD'S EYE

LOCATING A VANISHING POINT IN BIRD'S EYE

Using a scale plan position the vanishing point where you will see the best views from the customer viewpoint. Usually the centre of a major run of units.

Once you are happy with your VP just project all the visible lines UPWARDS and then determine the measurements you wish to use.

02   PREPARATION

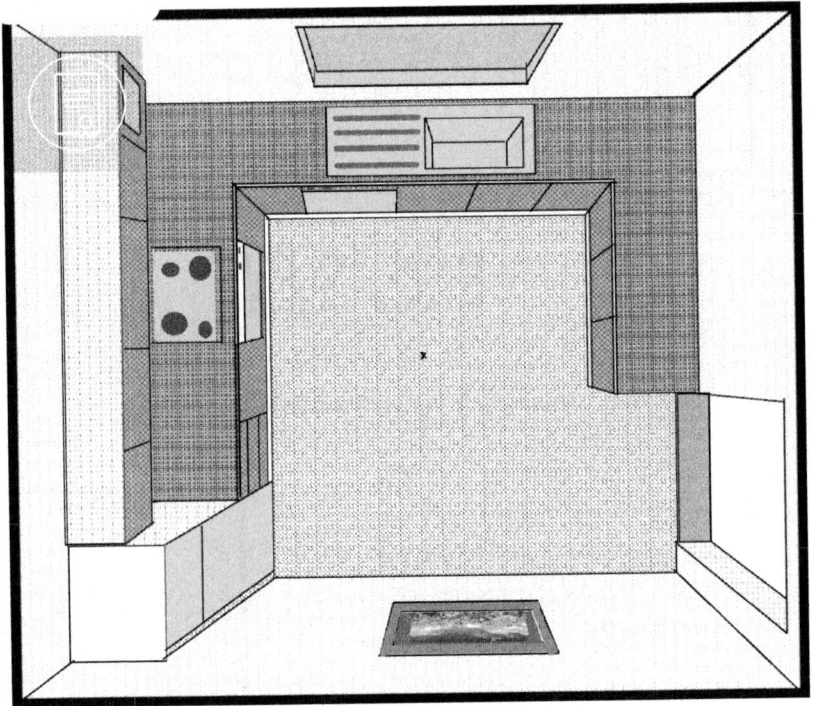

I would have hoped that you have by now perfected the other perspective and 3d drawing methods. Clearly, if this is the case you should have n o problem in following this guide. If you have not you may be struggling and I would urge you to study at least 2 of our guides to get a grasp of the basics and especially the perspective measurement techniques.

This wall transformed in 5 minutes to bird's eye

vanishing point

Transforming an existing scale plan

You can transform an existing plan directly or by tracing in just a few minutes. I sold hundreds of kitchens and bathrooms with this method. Average plan took 10-15 minutes and then made into a professional look by a tracer.

03

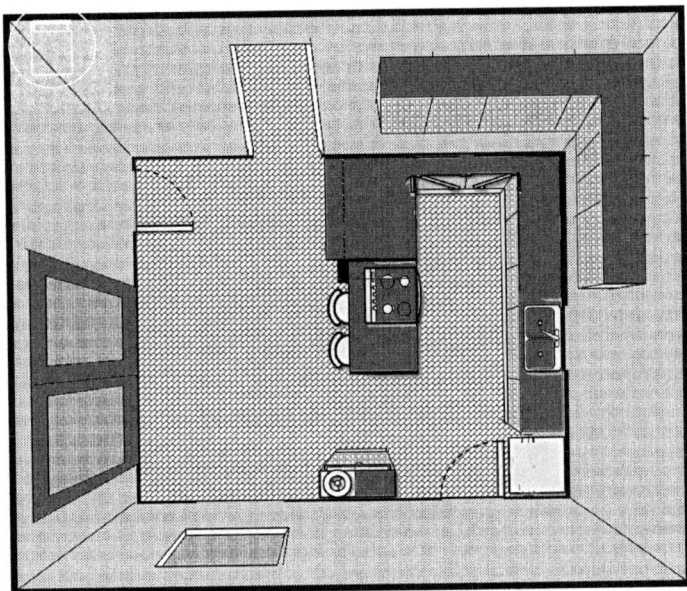

BIRDS' EYE METHOD

BIRDS' EYE METHOD

STEP BY STEP BASIC KITCHEN METHOD

• can be drawn directly from the original plan

• you can use all the lines of the plan but delete awkward detail.

• work directly from scale plan-all items on the worktop are in scale and can be drawn from stencils

• show all details of a large room.

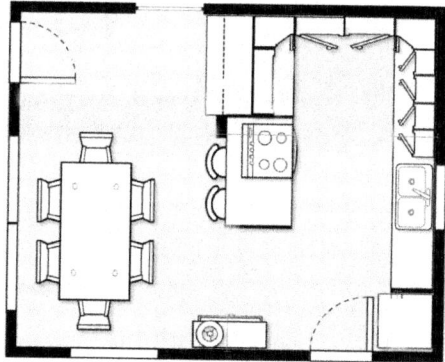

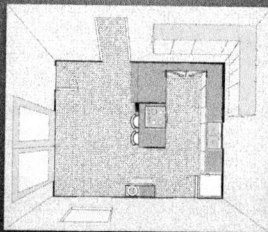

Birds Eye Convenient Method

Converting a formal plan to Birds Eye

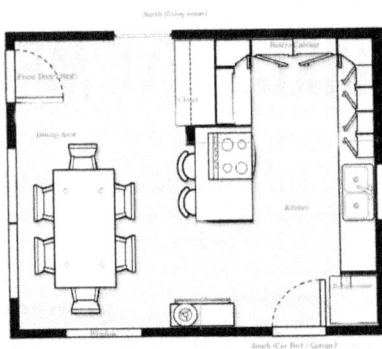

Step 1

take a scale plan

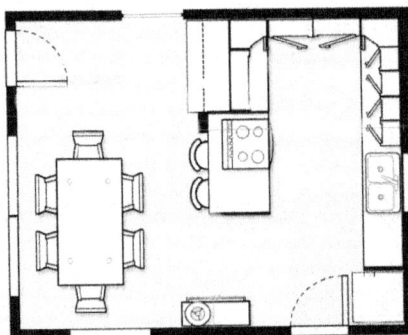

Step 2

simplify the plan

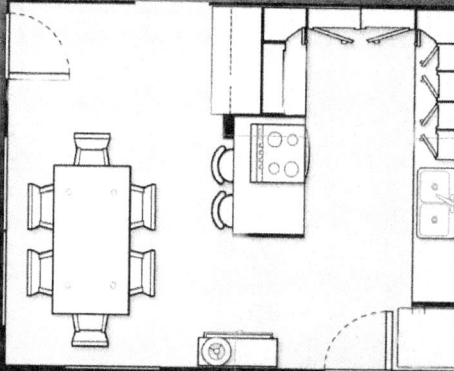

Step 3

reduce plan to outline only

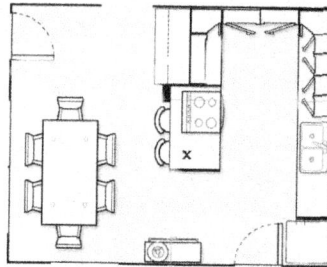

Step 4

Locate the vanishing point - you can select any position but best to choose one that gives the best view of the kitchen presentation

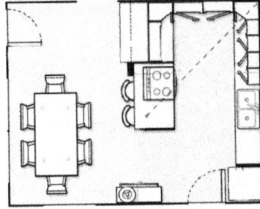

Step 5

line up the vanishing point
with the **room** corner

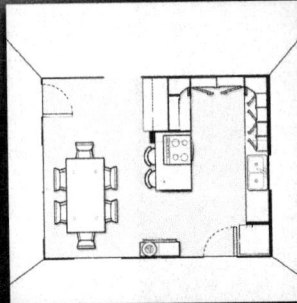

step 6

project all the corners of the
room using the vanishing point

Step 7

using the vanishing point project the
base units DOWN into the room and
the wall line UP into the room -
complete the outline as this stage

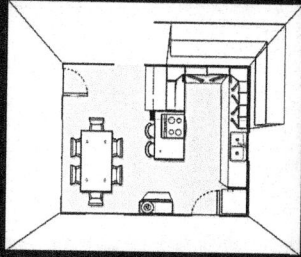

Step 8

tidy the room outline by deleting
items not required to work with and
the wall line plan lines - leaving a
clean birds eye outline with other
details such as french doors and
windows etc.

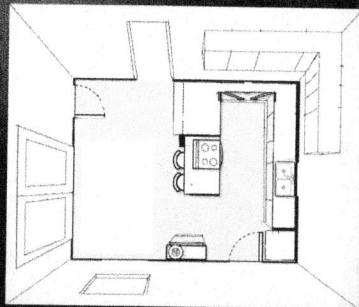

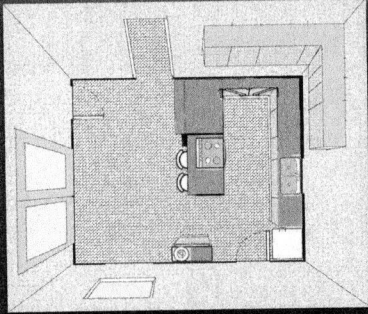

Add rendering and detail

you now have a credible birds eye presentation simply using your basic plan

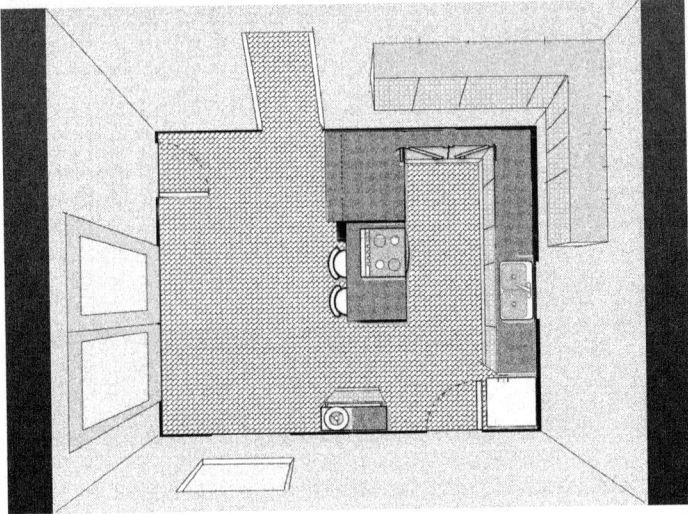

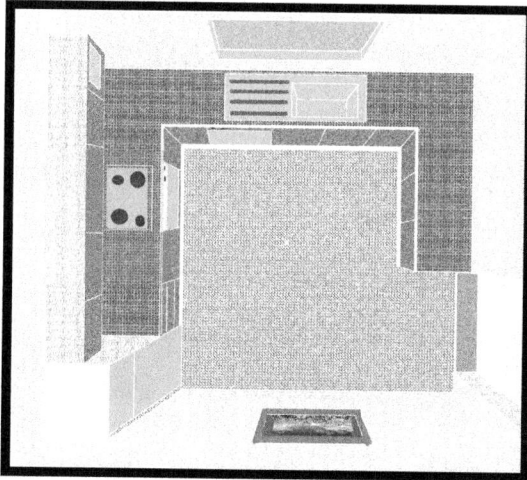

04

- still very simple and in scale.

- you can use your existing plan by tracing.

- all the benefits of using stencils and other aids.

BIRD'S EYE FORMAL METHOD

Bird's eye was one of the first techniques that I perfected something like 35 years ago. the big benefit is you can extend it directly from your scale plan simply by selecting your best vanishing point and using tracing paper. Now with any of the drawing programmes on a computer you can create your own very personal 3d view of the kitchen. Combining your drawing programme with a graphics programme you can also very simply and quickly render the finished item - quite effectively. And, of course any hand drawing technique can delivery really stunning results.

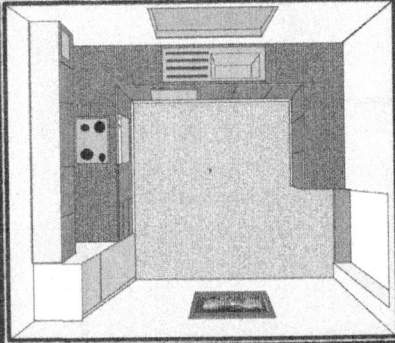

Bird's Eye Formal

Start from scratch - takes a little longer but very simple

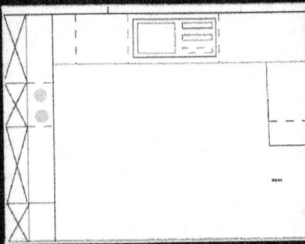

Step 1

☐ Start with a simple plan to scale

Step 2

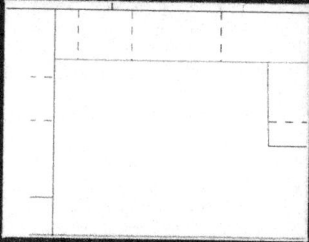

☐ Transfer the basic measurements to your birds eye project - perhaps using tracing paper or scanning.

Step 3

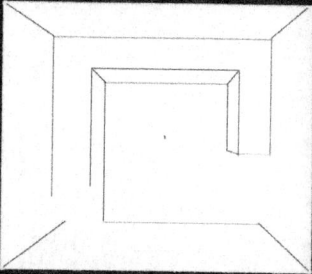

☐ after transferring the basic measurements select the vanishing point and then project the room corners and carcass outline from the measurements transferred

Step 4

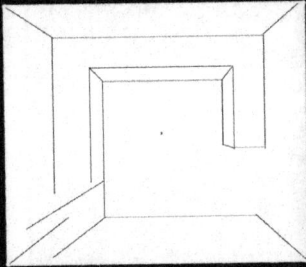

☐ Continue with the detail of carcassing outline for example outline the fridge unit.

Step 5

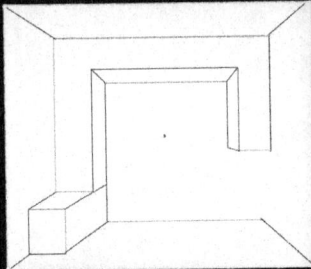

☐ Continue with the detailing and complete the floor standing carcassing

Step 6

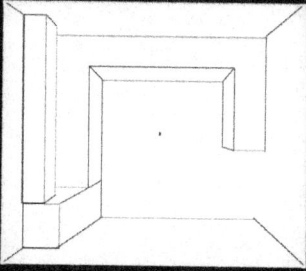

☐ Now complete the wall carcassing

Step 7

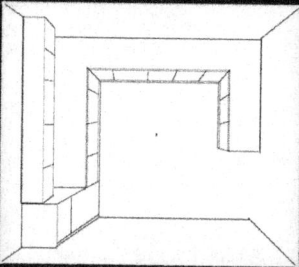

☐ now is a good time to transfer the individual unit doors

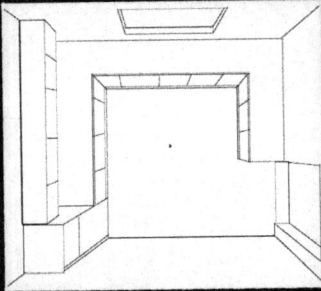

Step 8

- add more detail such as windows, fridge detail etc

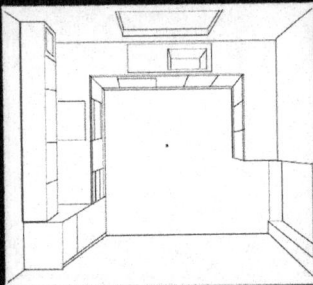

Step 9

- continue with detail for sink, appliances, glass door etc

Step 10

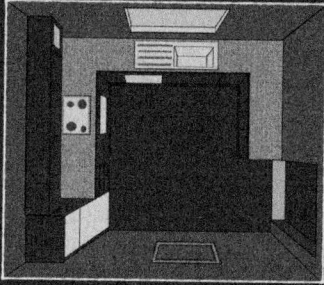

☐ introduce some rendering

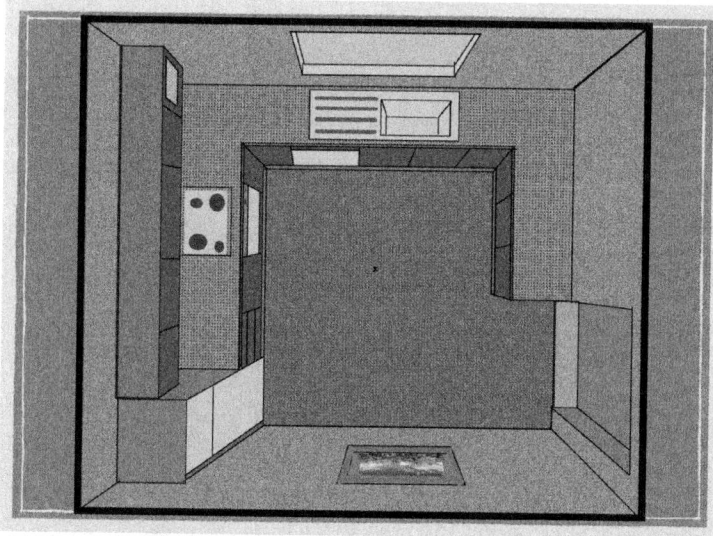

BIRD'S EYE BATHROOM METHOD

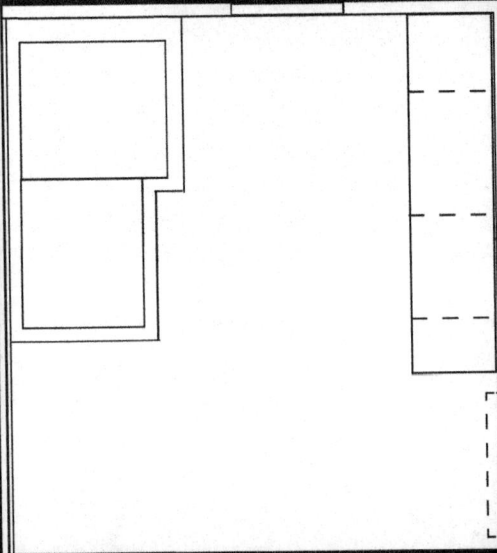

✓Drawn from a scale plan

✓many items are in scale

✓no complicated drawing techniques

✓can show the complete room.

Bird's Eye Bathroom Method

Step 2

start with your scale plan

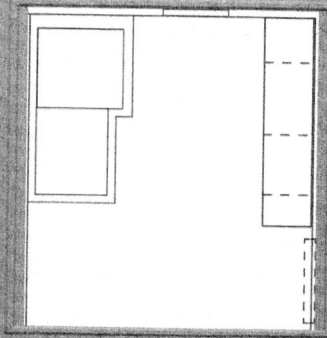

Step 3

project the 4corners of the
wall with your vanishing
point

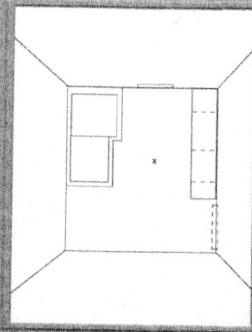

Step 3

start adding furnishings
sizes

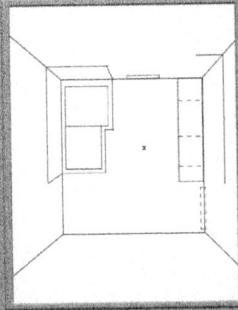

Step 4

continue with outlines and
remove other lines which
will be hidden

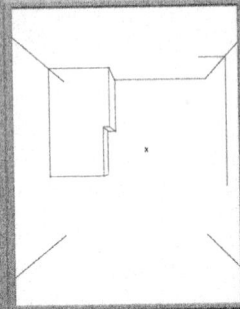

Step 5

continue with outlines

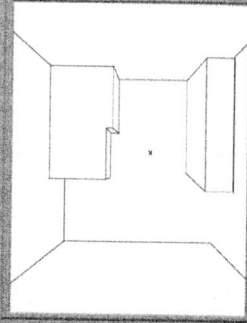

Step 6

continue with detail

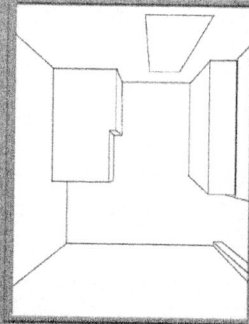

step 7

continue with detail ,
plinths etc and other details
as desired

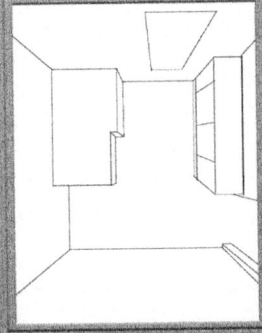

Step 8

add furnishing details

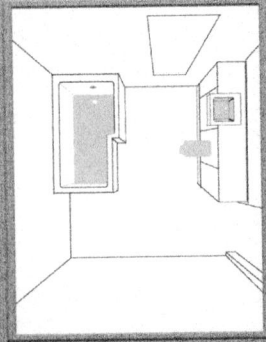

Step 9
continue building sanitary ware

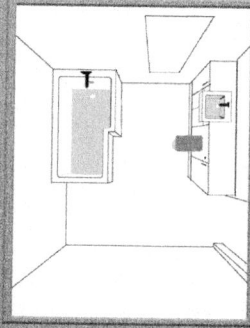

Step 10
completing the design details

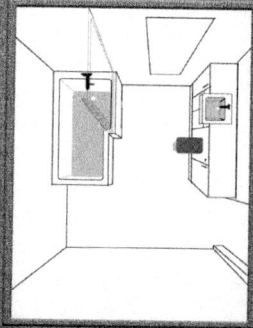

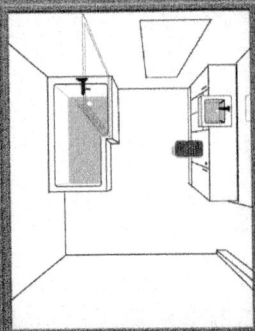

Step 11
adding final details

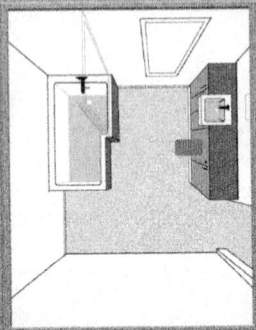

Step 12
start rendering

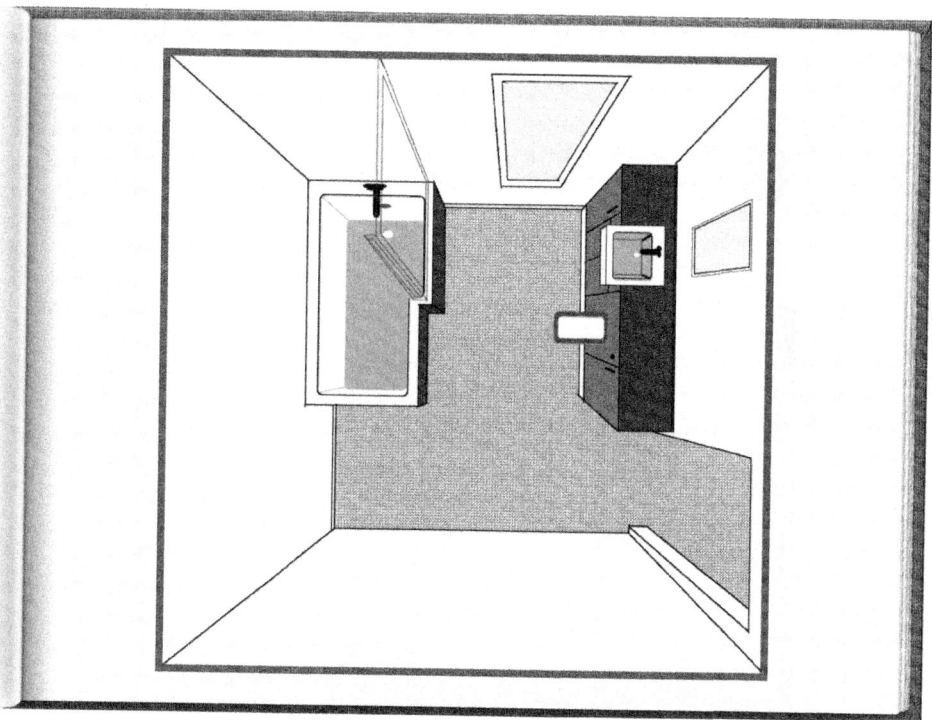

05

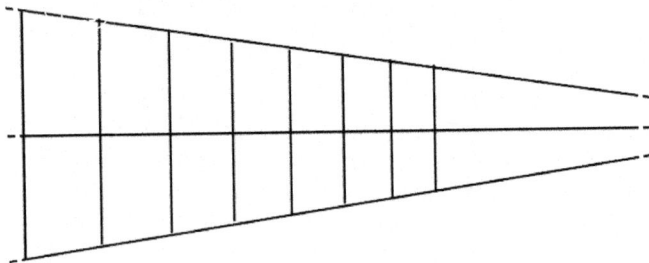

Perhaps produce your own ruler

In birds eye you start from your scale drawing. All vertical measurements are arbitrary so you can use anything; 1:50 is often convenient.

Use any system you want, - the perspective ruler is easiest but work on judgment for the long term

PERSPECTIVE MEASUREMENTS

5·0
6·0

4·5
5·4

1·2   1·8   2·4
1·0   1·5   2·0

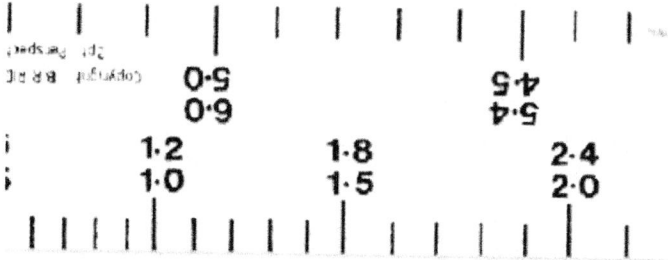

PERSPECTIVE RULER

You can just use a simple scale rule which you will find perfectly acceptable in any standard interior drawing. For larger rooms or exterior drawings you may wish to introduce an element of perspective variation but you will find this is not critical and you can quite easily guestimate the variation that looks best. Try measuring for a couple of drawings and then guestimating as you progress with the technique.

We covered this in previous guides but it is important & worth emphasising

The return wall or perspective measurements are the one single item that deters the assimilation of the various methods.

While you cannot ignore the subject we have found that if you simplify the determination of these measurements processes the learner can get on with the more important job at hand. As observed elsewhere in this book we have found that this subject is one that even professionals struggle with.

The best approach is to use whichever seems simpler to yourself and you will gradually build up your own understanding. The applies to all measurements that are not in true scale.

When developing the judgment system use larger and larger divisions on the ruler and then judge the intermediate measurements.

PERSPECTIVE RULER©

06

Bird's eye is excellent for those really big projects that you want to show a full presentation covering many aspects of your design.

A big kitchen

A kitchen diner

A large bedroom and en suite.

An entire floor of a house

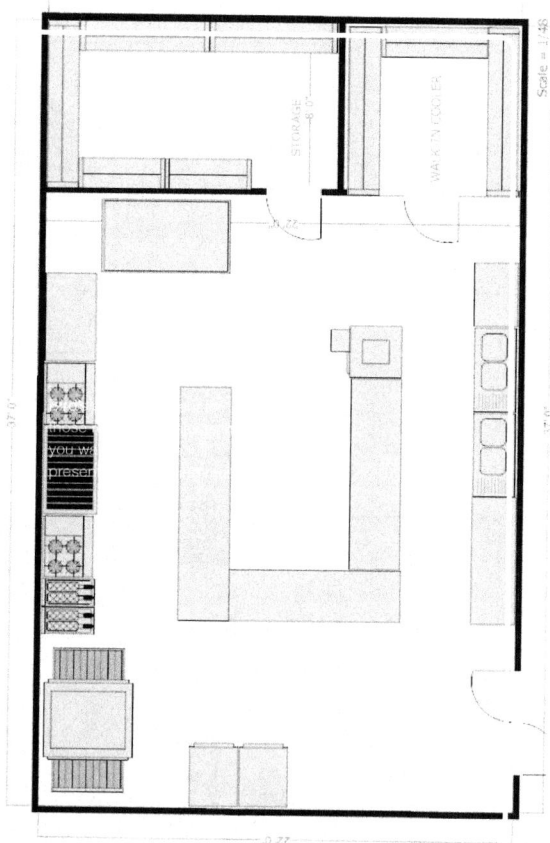

THE GRAND DESIGN

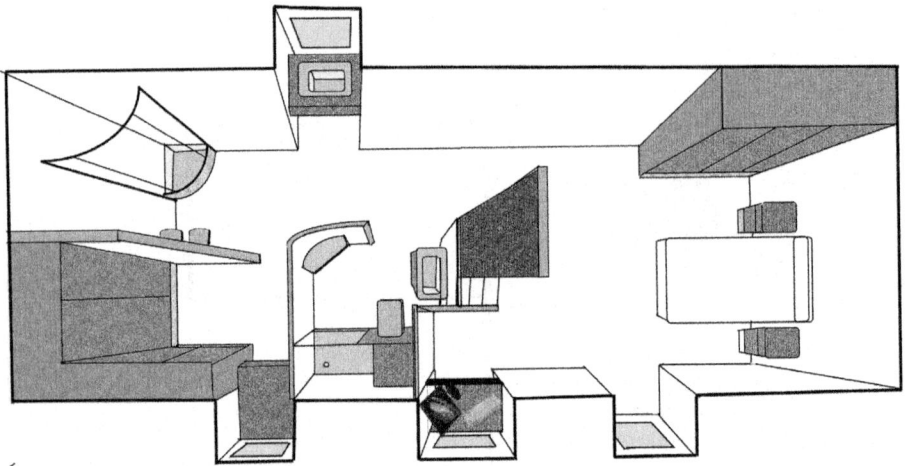
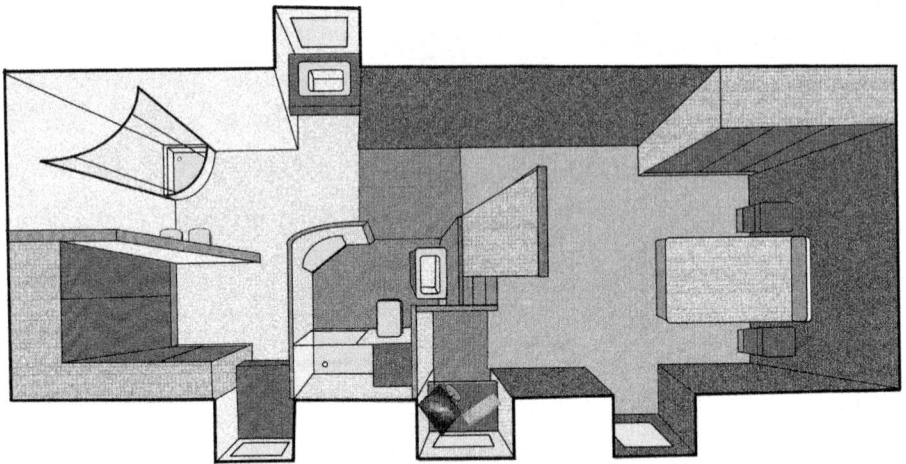

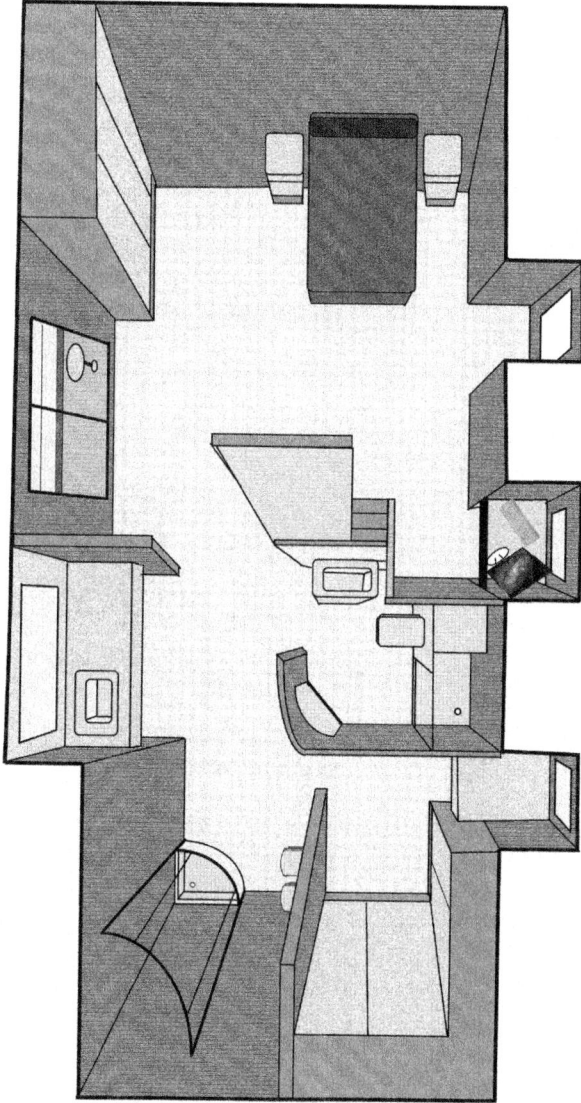

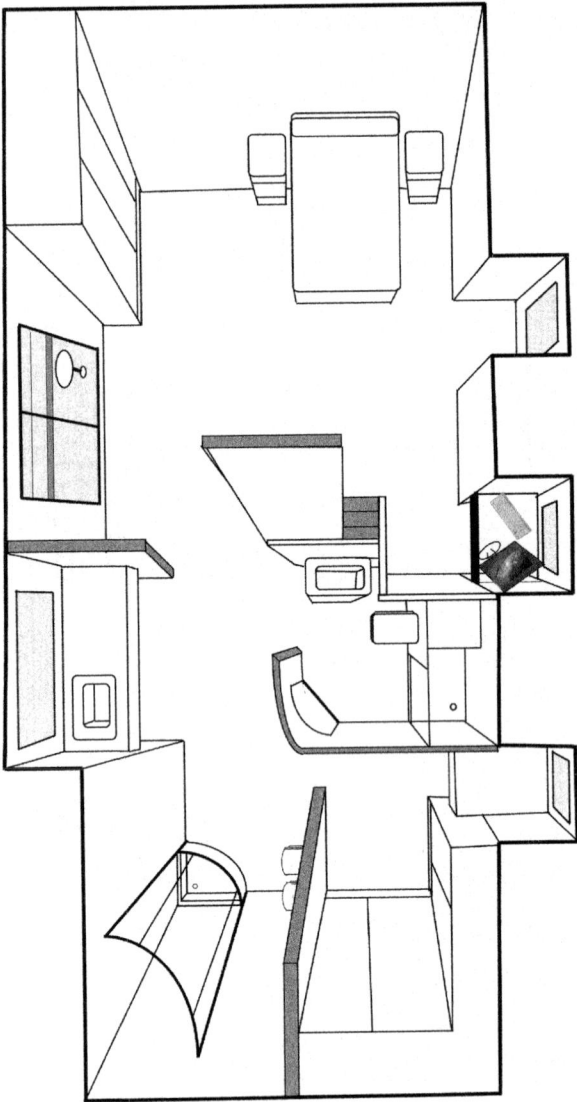

07

While the purists will want to see hand drawn efforts you can still produce quality drawings and rendering using a basic computer drawing programme, Often you will find that using two programmes might deliver the best results, for example Adobe Illustrator and Graphic Converter teamed together work well. With a bit of practice you will find CAD superfluous.

DRAWING WITH A COMPUTER

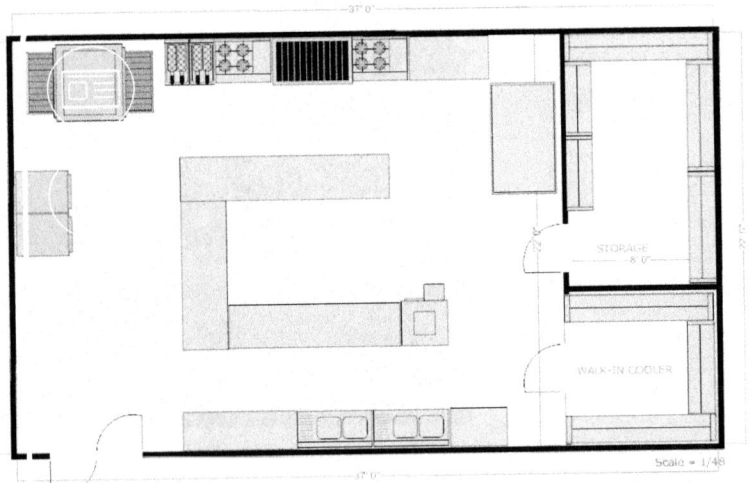

Scale = 1/48

✓ practrice a few step by step drawings first

✓ then draw this plan (full size next page) in bird's eye

✓ then produce a finished fully rendered presentation in a variety of trial finishes

EXERCISE

After you have practice this technique you should find it quite simple.

But it is important to practice. practice. practice.

Please note some elements of the plan are not completely clear so use your own interpretation.

You can also request further exercises by going to our support page and logging in and then completing your form.

SUPPORT

Thank you for purchasing this latest version of our bird's eye perspective guide.

We want you to enjoy this publication and learn from it,

To this end we offer TOTAL SUPPORT - if you feel you need help or clarification on any points please log in to our website at

www.kbb2000.com

Some current mini guide titles - not all are on general release if in doubt enquire on the website

KITCHEN PLANNING ESSENTIALS	I POINT PERSPECTIVE & VANISHING POINT	SURVEYING TECHNIQUES	EXTERIOR PRESENTATIONS
KITCHEN PLANNING APPLIANCES ESSENTIALS	2 POINT PERSPECTIVE & VANISHING POINT	GRANNY FLATS	CLOAK ROOMS DRESSING ROOMS CLOSETS
KITCHEN DESIGN	BIRDS EYE PERSPECTIVE	KITCHEN WORKING TRIANGLE	DOUBLE WORKING TRIANGLE
BATHROOM PLANNING	BEDROOM PRESENTATION	CREATIVE INTERIOR DESIGN USING A COMPUTER	CAD VS BRAIN
BATHROOM DESIGN	BATHROOM		

08

BIRD'S EYE?

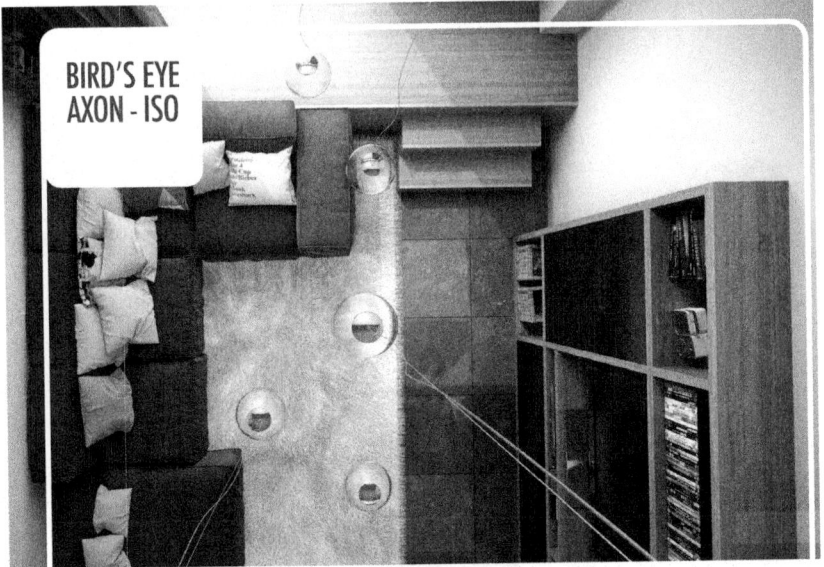

BIRD'S EYE
AXON - ISO

AT THIS STAGE YOU SHOULD REVIEW YOUR AXONOMETRIC AND ISOMETRIC 3D DRAWING GUIDE.

MANY OF THE PLANS AND IMAGES YOU SEE PUBLISHED AS BIRD'S EYE PRESENTATIONS ARE NOT NECESSARILY BIRD'S EYE PERSPECTIVE PRESENTATIONS. IN MANY CASES THEY ARE JUST CLASSIC AXONOMETRIC OR ISOMETRIC DRAWINGS OF LARGE HOUSES OR EXTERNAL STUDIES AND GARDEN PLANS. IN MANY CASES THEY ARE NOT WHOLLY TRUE AXONOMETRIC - ISOMETRIC OR BIRD'S EYE PERSPECTIVE BUT A COMBINATION OF THESE.

STUDY THE IMAGES ON THE FOLLOWING PAGES AND YOU SHOULD SEE WHAT WE MEAN AND BE ABLE TO PRODUCE YOUR OWN EXAMPLES PERHAPS FROM THE PREVIOUS EXERCISES.

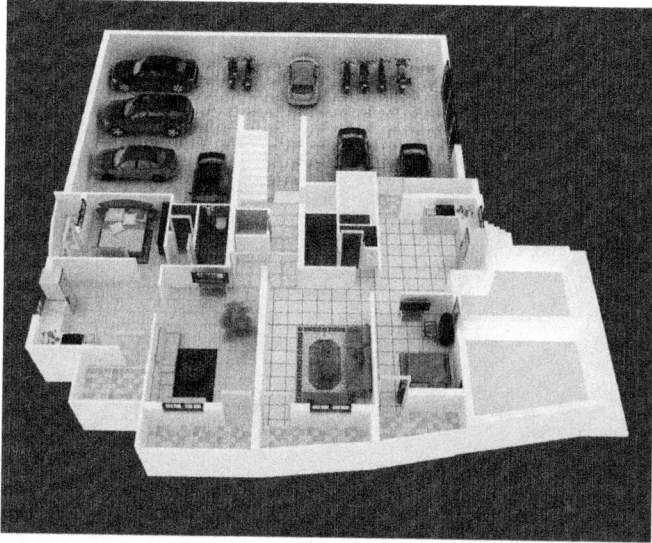

This is not a true perspective nor an axonometric/isometric drawing but a combination of the two and makes a very impressive presentation.

If you have been following the mini guides in order you should not we in a position to undertake your own drawings of this type. Have a go. If you haven't yet covered axonometric I would recommend you study asap.

for those of you studying bathrooms and interiors this is a genuine birds eye of a w.c. and you can easily follow the vanishing point.

You can also see that any object in true bird's eye is virtually in scale and only necessary to use a template and then follow the vanishing point for any 3d detail.

CPSIA information can be obtained
at www.ICGtesting.com
Printed in the USA
LVOW04s2146150117
521025LV00015B/788/P